The Life, Loves, and Lawsuits of a Legendary Victorian

BRIAN
THOMPSON

The Disastrous Mrs. Weldon